CAPE EDITIONS 1

General Editor: NATHANIEL TARN

The Scope of
Anthropology
Claude
Lévi-Strauss

Translated from the French by
Sherry Ortner Paul and Robert A. Paul

JONATHAN CAPE
THIRTY BEDFORD SQUARE
LONDON

Available in the United States from Grossman Publishers, Inc.

First published in Great Britain 1967
by Jonathan Cape Ltd, 30 Bedford Square, London WCI
Reprinted 1968, 1969, 1971
Translated from the French *Leçon Inaugurale*
This translation © 1967 by Jonathan Cape Ltd,
with acknowledgements to the Editor, *Current Anthropology*,
vol. 7, no. 2

CAPE Paperback edition ISBN 0 224 61271 9
        Hardback edition ISBN 0 224 61277 8

GROSSMAN Paperback edition SBN 670-62263-X
           Hardback edition SBN 670 62262-1

LCCC 68-55829

Printed and bound in Great Britain
by Richard Clay (The Chaucer Press), Ltd
Bungay, Suffolk

*The Scope of
Anthropology*

THE SCOPE OF ANTHROPOLOGY

Inaugural lecture, Chair of Social Anthropology,
Collège de France, January 5th, 1960

It was little more than a year ago, in 1958, that
the Collège de France took the decision to create in
its midst a chair of social anthropology. This science
is too susceptible to those forms of thought which,
when we encounter them among ourselves, we call
superstition, for me not to be allowed to render to
superstition an initial homage. Is it not the character
of myths, which have such an important place in
our research, to evoke a suppressed past and to apply
it, like a grid, upon the present in the hope of discovering a sense in which the two aspects of his own
reality man is confronted with – the historic and the
structural – coincide? Let me also be allowed on this
occasion, in the course of which all the features of
myth are for me reunited, to proceed on their example, seeking to discern in a number of past events
the meaning and the lesson of the honour which has
been done me. The very date of your deliberation, my
dear colleagues, bears witness – by the strange re-
currence of the number 8, already well known from
the arithmetic of Pythagoras, the periodic table of
chemical elements, and the law of symmetry of the
medusa-jelly fish – that the proposal in 1958 to create

a chair of social anthropology revives a tradition which even if I had wished to I would not have been able to escape.

Fifty years prior to your initial decision, Sir James George Frazer delivered at the University of Liverpool the inaugural lecture of the first chair in the world ever to be devoted to social anthropology. Fifty years earlier, in 1858, two men were born – Franz Boas and Émile Durkheim – whom posterity will regard as, if not the founders, at least the chief engineers, one in America and the other in France, of anthropology as we know it today.

It is appropriate that these anniversaries, these names, have been evoked here. Those of Frazer and Boas give me occasion to express my gratitude, if only briefly, for all that social anthropology owes to Anglo-American thought, and for what I owe it personally, since it was in close conjunction with it that my first endeavours were conceived and developed. But it will not surprise you that Durkheim occupies a larger place in this lecture. He incarnates the essence of France's contribution to social anthropology, even though his centennial, celebrated with enthusiasm in many foreign countries, passed almost unnoticed here and has not yet been marked by any official ceremony.[1]

How are we to explain this injustice done to him, and to ourselves, if not as a minor consequence of that desperate eagerness which drives us to forget our own history, to hold it 'in horror', in the words of Charles de Rémusat? This sentiment today renders

[1] A commemoration took place at the Sorbonne on January 30th, 1960.

social anthropology liable to the possibility of losing Durkheim as it has already lost Gobineau and Demeunier.

And yet, my dear colleagues, those among you who share these distant memories will not contradict me if I recall that, around 1935, when our Brazilian friends wanted to explain to us the reasons which led them to choose French missions for the organization of their first universities, they always cited the names: first, of course, Pasteur, and after that Durkheim.

But in reserving these thoughts for Durkheim, I am carrying out another duty. No one would have appreciated more than Marcel Mauss an homage addressed to him at the same time as to the master of whom he was pupil and then successor. From 1931 to 1942, Marcel Mauss held the chair at the Collège de France devoted to the study of society, and so brief was the passage in these halls of the unfortunate Maurice Halbwachs, it seems that one can, within the bounds of truth, consider that in creating a chair of social anthropology, it is Mauss's chair which you wanted to restore. In any case, I owe too much to Mauss's thought not to take pleasure in this speculation.

To be sure, his chair was called 'Sociology', for Mauss, who did so much (together with Paul Rivet) to make anthropology a science in its own right, had not completely succeeded by the 1930s. But to attest to the continuity between our teaching, it will suffice to recall that in Mauss's field anthropology assumed an ever-growing place; that beginning in 1924, he proclaimed that the 'place of sociology' was 'in

9

anthropology';[1] and that, if I am not mistaken, Mauss was the first (in 1938) to introduce the term 'social anthropology' into French terminology.[2] He would not disavow the term today.

Even in his boldest theoretical departures, Mauss never felt that he had moved far from the Durkheimian line. Better than he, perhaps, we perceive today how, without betraying the loyalty he so often reaffirmed, Mauss knew how to simplify and make more pliable the doctrine of his great precursor. This doctrine has never ceased to astonish us by its imposing proportions and its powerful logical framework, and by the perspectives which it opened on to horizons where so much remains to be explored. Mauss's mission was to finish and furnish the prodigious edifice conjured from the earth at the passage of the demiurge. He had to exorcize some metaphysical phantoms that were still trailing their chains in it, and shelter it once and for all from the icy winds of dialectic, the thunder of syllogisms, and the lightning flashes of antinomies. But Mauss secured the Durkheimian school against yet other dangers.

Durkheim was probably the first to introduce the requirement of specificity into the sciences of man, thereby opening the way for a renovation from which most of these sciences, and especially linguistics, benefited at the beginning of the twentieth century. In all

[1] 'Rapports réels et pratiques de la psychologie et de la sociologie', in *Sociologie et Anthropologie* (Paris, 1950), p. 285.
[2] 'Une catégorie de l'esprit humaine: La Notion de personne', ibid., p. 362.

forms of human thought and activity, one cannot ask questions regarding nature or origin before having identified and analysed phenomena and discovered to what extent their interrelations suffice to explain them. It is impossible to discuss an object, to reconstruct the process of its coming into being without knowing first *what it is*; in other words, without having exhausted the inventory of its internal determinants.

Yet on re-reading *The Rules of Sociological Method* today, one cannot help thinking that Durkheim has applied these principles with a certain partiality; he appeals to them in order to constitute the social as an independent category, but without recognizing that this new category, in its turn, entails all sorts of specificities corresponding to the different aspects through which we apprehend it. Before demanding that logic, language, law, art and religion be considered as projections of the social, would it not have been reasonable to wait until the particular sciences had thoroughly explored the mode of organization and the differential function of each of these codes, thus permitting the understanding of their interrelations?

At the risk of being accused of paradox, it seems to me that in the theory of the 'total social fact' (so often praised and so poorly understood), the notion of totality is less important than the very special way in which Mauss conceived of it: foliated as it were and made up of a multitude of distinct yet connected planes. Instead of appearing as a postulate, the totality of the social is manifested in experience – privileged instances which one can apprehend on the level of observation, in well defined situations, when 'the totality of society and its institutions ... is set in motion.' Now, this totality does not suppress the specific character of phenomena, which remain 'at once juridical, economic, religious, and even aesthetic or morphological', so that totality consists finally in the network of functional interrelations among all these planes.[1]

This empirical attitude taken by Mauss accounts for the rapidity with which he overcame the repugnance Durkheim had felt from the beginning towards ethnographic investigation. 'What counts', said Mauss, 'is the Melanesian of such-and-such an island ...'[2] *Contra* the theoretician, the observer should always have the last word; and against the observer, the native. Finally, behind the rationalized interpretations of the native – who often makes himself into an observer and even theoretician of his own society – one will look for the 'unconscious categories' which, Mauss wrote in one of his first works, are determinants 'in magic, as in religion, as in linguistics'.[3] Now, this analysis in depth was to permit Mauss, without contradicting Durkheim (since it was to be on a new plane), to re-establish bridges – which at times had been imprudently destroyed – between his concerns and the other sciences of man: history, since the ethnographer deals in the particular, and also biology and psychology, since he recognized that social

[1] 'Essai sur le don: Forme et raison de l'échange dans les sociétés archaïques', in *Sociologie et Anthropologie* (Paris, 1950), p. 274.

[2] Ibid., p. 276.

[3] 'Esquisse d'une théorie générale de la magie', in *Sociologie et Anthropologie* (Paris, 1950), p. 111.

phenomena are 'first social, but also, and simulta-
neously, physiological and psychological'.[1] It will be
sufficient to take the analysis far enough to attain a
level where, again as Mauss said, 'body, soul, society –
everything merges'.[2]

This down-to-earth sociology studies men as they
are depicted by travellers and ethnographers who have
partaken of their existence either in a fleeting or in
a more permanent way. It shows them engaged in
their own historical development, settled in a concrete, geographical space. It has, says Mauss, 'as
principle and as goal ... to perceive the entire group
and the entire range of its behaviour'.[3]

If disembodiment was one of the perils which lay in
wait for Durkheimian sociology, Mauss protected it
with equal success against another danger: automatically guaranteed explanation. Too often since
Durkheim – and even among some of those who believe themselves to be liberated from his doctrinal
grip – sociology had seemed like the product of a
raid hastily carried out at the expense of history,
psychology, linguistics, economics, law and ethno-
graphy. To the booty of this pillage, sociology was
content to add its own labels; whatever problem was
submitted to it could be assured of receiving a pre-
fabricated 'sociological' solution.

We owe it in large part to Mauss and to Malinowski
that we are no longer at that stage. At the same
moment and no doubt aided by one another, they

[1] 'Rapports réels et pratiques de la psychologie et de la
sociologie', in Sociologie et Anthropologie (Paris, 1950), p. 299.
[2] Ibid., p. 302.
[3] 'Essai sur le don'. p. 276.

showed – Mauss as theoretician, Malinowski as experimenter – what could constitute proof in the anthropological sciences. They were first to understand clearly that it was not enough to break down and dissect. Social facts do not reduce themselves to scattered fragments. They are lived by men, and subjective consciousness is as much a form of their reality as their objective characteristics.

While Malinowski was instituting the ethnographer's uncompromising participation in the life and thought of the natives, Mauss was affirming that what is essential 'is that movement of all, the living aspect, the fleeting instant in which society becomes or in which men become, sentimentally conscious of themselves and of their situation vis-à-vis others'.[1] This empirical and subjective synthesis offers the only possible guarantee that the preliminary analysis, carried as far as the unconscious categories, has allowed nothing to escape.

Without a doubt, the attempt will remain largely illusory : we shall never know if the other, into whom we cannot, after all, dissolve, fashions from the elements of his social existence a synthesis exactly superimposable on that which we have worked out. But it is not necessary to go so far; all we need – and for this, inner understanding suffices – is that the synthesis, however approximate, arises from human experience. We must be sure of this, since we study men; and as we are ourselves men, we have that possibility. The way in which Mauss poses and resolves the problem in his *Essay on the Gift*[2] exhibits, in the

[1] 'Essai sur le don', p. 275.
[2] P. 285.

intersection of his subjectivities, the nearest order of truth to which the sciences of man can aspire when they confront this object integrally.

Let us make no mistake: all this which seemed so new was implicit in Durkheim. He has often been reproached for having formulated, in the second part of *The Elementary Forms of the Religious Life*, a theory of religion so vast and so general that it seemed to render superfluous the minute analysis of Australian religions which preceded it and – one would have hoped – paved the way for it.

The problem is to know if Durkheim the human being could have arrived at this theory without being forced, at the outset, to superimpose upon the religious representations his own society had taught him those of men whom historical and geographical evidence guaranteed to have been entirely 'others', not accomplices or unsuspected acolytes. Such is certainly the approach of the ethnographer when he goes into the field, for, however scrupulous and objective he may want to be, it is never either himself or the other whom he encounters at the end of his investigation. At most he can claim to extricate, by the superposition of himself on the other, what Mauss called the facts of general functioning, which he showed were more universal and had even more reality.

In thus completing the intentions of Durkheim, Mauss liberated anthropology from the false opposition (introduced by thinkers such as Dilthey and Spengler) between explanation in the physical sciences and explanation in the human sciences. The search for causes ends with the assimilation of an experience, but this is at once external and internal. The famous injunction to 'consider social facts as things' corresponds to the first step, the search for causes, which are left to the second to validate. We already discern the originality of social anthropology: it consists not in opposing casual explanation and understanding, but in bringing to light an object which may be at the same time objectively very remote and subjectively very concrete, and whose casual explanation may be based on that understanding which is, for us, but a supplementary form of proof. A notion like that of empathy inspires great mistrust in us, because it connotes an added dose of irrationalism and mysticism. In his demand for additional proof, we prefer to imagine the anthropologist modelled after the engineer, who conceives and constructs a machine by a series of rational operations: it has to work; logical certainty is not enough. The possibility of trying the intimate experiences of another upon oneself is but one of the means at one's disposal for obtaining that final empirical satisfaction for which the physical sciences and the human sciences feel an equal necessity: it is less a proof, perhaps, than a guarantee.

What, then, is social anthropology? No one, it seems to me, was closer to defining it – if only by virtually disregarding its existence – than Ferdinand de Saussure, when, introducing linguistics as part of a science yet to be born, he reserved for this science the name *semiology* and attributed to it as its object of study the life of signs at the heart of social life.

Did he not, furthermore, anticipate our adherence when he compared language to 'writing, to the alphabet of deaf-mutes, to symbolic rites, to forms of politeness, to military signals, etc.'?[1] No one would deny that anthropology numbers within its own field at least some of these systems of signs, along with many others: mythical language, the oral and gestural signs of which ritual is composed, marriage rules, kinship systems, customary laws, and certain terms and conditions of economic exchange.

I conceive, then, of anthropology as the bona-fide occupant of that domain of semiology which linguistics has not already claimed for its own, pending the time when for at least certain sections of this domain, special sciences are established within anthropology.

It is necessary, however, to make this definition more precise in two ways.

First of all, I hasten to recognize that certain items which have just been cited are already within the scope of particular sciences: economics, law, political science. However, these disciplines examine the very facts which are closest to us as anthropologists and are thus of particular interest. Let us say that social anthropology apprehends these facts, either in their most distant manifestations, or from the angle of their most general expression. From this latter point of view, anthropology can do nothing useful without collaborating closely with the particular social sciences; but these, for their part, would not know how to aspire to generality were it not for the co-operation of anthropology, which alone is capable of

[1] *Cours de linguistique générale* (Paris, 1960), p. 33.

bringing them the accounts and the inventories which it seeks to render complete.

The second difficulty is more serious, because one can ask oneself whether all the phenomena in which social anthropology is interested really do manifest themselves as signs. This is sufficiently clear for the problems we study most frequently. When we consider some system of belief (let us say totemism), some form of social organization (unilineal clans, bilateral cross-cousin marriage), the question which we ask ourselves is indeed, 'What does all this mean or *signify*?', and to answer it, we force ourselves to *translate* into our language rules originally stated in a different code.

But is this true of other aspects of social reality, such as a stock of tools, various techniques, and modes of production and of consumption? It would seem that we are concerned here with objects, not with signs – the sign being, according to Peirce's celebrated definition, 'that which replaces something for someone'. What, then, does a stone axe replace and for whom?

The objection is valid up to a certain point, and it explains the repugnance which some people feel towards admitting phenomena which come from other sciences, such as geography and technology, into the field of social anthropology. The term 'cultural anthropology' will be appropriate, then, to distinguish and defend the originality of this part of our studies.

It is well known, however – and it is one of Mauss's claims to fame to have established this, along with Malinowski – that in the societies with which we are concerned above all, though not in them alone, these techniques are pregnant with meaning. From this point of view, they still concern us.

Finally, the intention of being exhaustive which inspires our researches very much transforms their object. Techniques taken in isolation may appear as raw fact, historical heritage, or the result of a compromise between human needs and the constraints of environment. They re-emerge in a new light, however, when one puts them back into that general inventory of societies which anthropology is trying to construct, for then we imagine them as the equivalents of choices which each society seems to make (I here use convenient language, which must be stripped of its anthropomorphism) among the possible ones which will constitute the complete list. In this sense, a certain type of stone axe can be a sign: in a given context, for the observer capable of understanding its use, it takes the place of the different implement which another society employs for the same purpose.

Consequently, then, even the simplest techniques of any primitive society have hidden in them the character of a system, analysable in terms of a more general system. The manner in which some elements of this system have been retained and others excluded permits us to conceive of the local system as a totality of significant choices, compatible or incompatible with other choices, which each society, or each period within its development, has been led to make.

In admitting the symbolic nature of its object, social

anthropology does not thereby intend to cut itself off from *realia*. How could it do this, when art, in which all is sign, utilizes material media? One cannot study the gods without knowing their icons; rites, without analysing the objects and the substances which the officiant makes or manipulates; social rules independently of the things which correspond to them. Social anthropology does not confine itself to a part of the domain of ethnology; it does not separate material and spiritual culture. In its own perspective, which we shall have to define, it devotes the same interest to each. If men communicate by means of symbols and signs, then, for anthropology, which is a conversation of man with man, everything is symbol and sign, when it acts as intermediary between two subjects.

By this deference towards objects and techniques, as well as by the conviction that we must work on meanings, social anthropology takes an appreciable degree of leave from Radcliffe-Brown who – right up to his untimely death in 1955 – did so much to give autonomy to our science.

According to the English master's wonderfully fluent opinions, social anthropology is to be an inductive science which, like other sciences of this type, observes facts, formulates hypotheses, and submits these to experimental control, in order to discover general laws of nature and society. It thus sets itself apart from ethnology, which tries to reconstruct the past of primitive societies, but with means and methods so precarious that it can teach social anthropology nothing.

When it was formulated, around 1940, this conception – inspired by the Durkheimian distinction be-tween *circumfusa* and *praeterita* – heralded a salutary reaction to the abuses of the diffusionist school. Since then, however, 'conjectural history', as Radcliffe-Brown called it, not without contempt, has perfected and refined its methods, thanks especially to strati-graphic excavations, the introduction of statistics into archaeology, the analysis of pollens, of the use of carbon-14, and above all, the even closer collabora-tion between ethnologists and sociologists, on the one hand, and archaeologists and prehistorians, on the other. One may well ask oneself, then, if Radcliffe-Brown's mistrust of historical reconstructions did not correspond to a stage of scientific development which we will soon have outdistanced.

On the other hand, several of us hold more modest views on the future of social anthropology than those which were encouraged by the great ambitions of Radcliffe-Brown. Such views picture social anthro-pology not on the model of the inductive sciences as they were conceived of in the nineteenth century, but rather as a taxonomy, whose purpose is to identify and to classify types, to analyse their constituent parts, and to establish correlations between them. Without this preliminary work – which, let us make no mis-take, has barely begun – the comparative method recommended by Radcliffe-Brown can only mark time : either the facts which one proposes to compare are so close to each other geographically or historically that one is never certain of dealing with distinct phenomena, or they are too heterogeneous, and the comparison must be considered illegitimate because it brings together things which one cannot compare.

Until a few years ago, we assumed that the aristocratic institutions of Polynesia were recent introductions: the result of the arrival of small groups of foreign conquerors only a few centuries ago. Now the measurement of residual radioactivity in organic remains from Melanesia and Polynesia reveals that the difference between the dates of occupation of the two regions is less than was supposed. All at once, conceptions about the nature and homogeneity of the feudal system must be modified; for at least in this part of the world, it can no longer be denied, after Guiart's excellent research, that such a system existed prior to the arrival of the conquerors, and that certain forms of feudalism can arise in humble gardening societies.[1]

The discovery in Africa of the art of Ife, as refined and sophisticated as that of the European Renaissance, but perhaps earlier by three or four centuries, and preceded in Africa itself by the much more ancient art of the so-called Nok civilization, influences our conceptions of the recent arts of Negro Africa and the corresponding cultures. We are now tempted to see them as impoverished, rustic replicas of high art forms and civilizations.

The shortening of the prehistory of the Old World and the lengthening of that of the New, which carbon-14 dating allows us to predict, will perhaps lead us to decide that the civilizations which developed on the two sides of the Pacific were even more akin to

[1] *L'organisation sociale et politique du Nord Malekula* (Nouméa: Institut français d'Océanie, 1963), and *Structure de la Chefferie en Melanésie du Sud* (Institut d'Ethnologie, Paris, 1963).

22

each other than they seem and to understand them differently, each on its own terms.

We must busy ourselves with facts of this order before tackling any classification or comparison. For if we hasten overmuch to postulate the homogeneity of the social field, while cherishing the illusion that it is immediately comparable in all its aspects and on all its levels, we will lose sight of essentials. We shall fail to appreciate that the co-ordinates required for defining two apparently very similar phenomena are not always the same in nature or number; and we shall believe we are formulating sociological laws when in fact we are only describing superficial properties or setting forth tautologies.

Scorning the historical dimension on the pretext that we have insufficient means to evaluate it, except approximately, will result in our being satisfied with an impoverished sociology, in which phenomena are set loose, as it were, from their foundations. Rules and institutions, states and processes seem to float in a void in which one strains to spread a tenuous network of functional relations. One becomes wholly absorbed in this task and forgets the men in whose thought these relationships are established, one neglects their material culture, one no longer knows whence they came and what they are.

Anthropology, indeed, should be in no hurry to claim as its own any phenomena liable to be called social. Espinas, another of the masters we allow ourselves the luxury of forgetting, was certainly right from the point of view of social anthropology when he refused to accept the notion that institutions without biological roots have the same coefficient of reality as others: 'The management of a great railroad company', he wrote in 1901, 'is not a social reality at all ... nor is an army.'[1]

The statement is excessive in so far as managements are subjected to thorough studies in sociology, in social psychology, and in other specialized sciences; but it helps us to specify the difference between anthropology and these other disciplines: the social facts which we study are manifested in societies each of which is a *total entity, concrete and cohesive*. We never lose sight of the fact that existing societies are the result of great transformations occurring in mankind at certain moments in prehistory and at certain places on the globe, and that an uninterrupted chain of real events relates these facts to those which we can observe.

The chronological and spatial continuity between the natural order and the cultural order upon which Espinas insisted strongly (in a language which is no longer our own and which, for that reason, we have trouble in understanding sometimes) is also the basis of Boas' historicism. It explains why anthropology, even social anthropology, claims to belong to the same area of concern as physical anthropology, whose discoveries it awaits almost eagerly. For, even if social phenomena ought to be provisionally isolated from the rest and treated as if they arose from a specific level, we know well that, both *de facto* and *de jure*, the emergence of culture will remain a mystery to man. Such a mystery will remain until he succeeds in determining, on the biological level, the modifica-

[1] 'Être ou ne pas être, ou le postulat de la sociologie', in *Revue Philosophique* I (1901), p. 470.

tions of the structure and functioning of the brain of which culture was at one and the same time the natural result and the social mode of apprehension, and which at the same time created the intersubjective milieu indispensable to further transformations. These transformations, although certainly anatomical and physiological, can be neither defined nor studied with reference to the individual alone.

This historian's profession of faith may come as a surprise, since I have at times been criticized for being uninterested in history and for paying scant attention to it in my work. I do not practise it much, but I am determined that its rights should be reserved. I merely believe that in this formative period of social anthropology, nothing would be more dangerous than an unmethodical eclecticism seeking to give the illusion of a finished science by confusing its tasks and mixing its programmes.

Now it happens that in anthropology, experimentation precedes both observation and hypothesis. One of the peculiarities of the small societies which we study is that each constitutes, as it were, a ready-made experiment, because of its relative simplicity and the limited number of variables required to explain its functioning. On the other hand, these societies are alive, and we have neither the time nor the means to manipulate them. By comparison with the natural sciences, we benefit from an advantage and suffer an inconvenience; we find our experiments already prepared but they are uncontrollable. It is therefore understandable that we attempt to replace them with models, systems of symbols which preserve the characteristic properties of the experiment, but which we can manipulate.

The boldness of such an approach is, however, compensated for by the humility – one might almost say the servility – of observation as it is practised by the anthropologist. Leaving his country and his home for long periods; exposing himself to hunger, sickness and occasional danger; allowing his habits, his beliefs, his convictions to be tampered with, conniving at this, indeed, when, without mental reservations or ulterior motives, he assumes the modes of life of a strange society, the anthropologist practises total observation, beyond which there is nothing except – and there *is* a risk – the complete absorption of the observer by the object of his observations.

This alternation between two methods (each involving its rhythm) – the deductive and the empirical – and the strictness with which we practise each in its extreme and most refined form give social anthropology its distinctive character : of all the sciences, it is without a doubt unique in making the most intimate subjectivity into a means of objective demonstration. We really can verify that the same mind which has abandoned itself to the experience and allowed itself to be moulded by it becomes the theatre of mental operations which, without suppressing the experience, nevertheless transform it into a model which releases further mental operations. In the last analysis, the logical coherence of these mental operations is based on the sincerity and honesty of the person who can say, like the explorer bird of the fable, 'I was there; such-and-such happened to me; you will believe you were there yourself,' and who in fact succeeds in communicating that conviction.

But this constant oscillation between theory and observation requires that the two levels always remain distinct. To return to history, it seems to me that the same holds true, whether one devotes oneself to the static or to the dynamic, to the order of the structure or to the order of the event. The history of the historians requires no defence, but we do not endanger it by saying (as Braudel admits) that next to a short span there exists a long span; that certain facts arise from a statistical and irreversible time, others from a mechanical and reversible time; and that the idea of a structural history contains nothing which could shock historians.[1] The two come together, and it is not contradictory that a history of symbols and ✳ signs engenders unforeseeable developments, even though it brings into play a limited number of structural combinations. In a kaleidoscope, each recombination of identical elements yields new results; but it is because the history of the historians is present – in the succession of flicks of the finger, as it were, which bring about the reorganization of the structure – and because the chances are practically nil that the same configuration will appear twice.

I do not mean, then, to take up again, in its original form, the distinction introduced in the *Course in General Linguistics* between the synchronic and the diachronic orders. From this aspect of the Saussurian doctrine, modern structuralism, along with Trubetz-

[1] 'Histoire et sciences sociales: la longue durée', in *Annales, Économies, Sociétés, Civilisations* (1954).

koy and Jakobson, has most energetically diverged; and recent documents show the extent to which the editors of the *Course* may at times have forced and schematized the master's thought.[1]

For the editors of the *Course in General Linguistics*, there exists an absolute opposition between two categories of fact : on the one hand, that of grammar, the synchronic, the conscious; on the other hand, that of the phonetic, the diachronic, the unconscious. Only the conscious system is coherent; the unconscious infra-system is dynamic and off-balance, composed at once of elements from the past and as yet unrealized future tendencies.

In fact, de Saussure had not yet discovered the presence of differential elements behind the phoneme. His position indirectly foreshadowed, on another plane, that of Radcliffe-Brown, who was convinced that structure is of the order of empirical observation, when in fact it lies beyond it. This ignorance of hidden realities leads the two men to opposite conclusions. De Saussure appears to deny the existence of a structure where it is not immediately given; Radcliffe-Brown confirms such an existence but, locating it in the wrong place, deprives the notion of structure of its full force and significance.

In anthropology, as in linguistics, we know today that the synchronic can be as unconscious as the diachronic. In this sense the divergence between the two is already reduced.

On the other hand, the *Course in General Linguistics* sets forth relations of equivalence between the

[1] R. Godel, *Les sources manuscrites du cours de linguistique générale de Ferdinand de Saussure* (Geneva, 1957).

phonetic, the diachronic, and the individual, which
pertain to speech (*parole*); and the grammatical, the
synchronic, and the collective, which pertain to
language (*la langue*). But we have learned from Marx
that the diachronic can also exist in the collective,
and from Freud that the grammatical can be achieved
entirely within the individual.

Neither the editors of the *Course* nor Radcliffe-
Brown sufficiently realized that the history of symbolic systems includes logical evolutions which relate
to different levels of the structural process and which
it is necessary first to isolate. If a conscious system
exists, it can only result from a sort of 'dialectical
average' among a multiplicity of unconscious systems, each of which concerns one aspect or one level
of social reality. Now, these systems do not coincide
either in their logical structures or in their historical
affiliations. They are as if diffracted upon a temporal
dimension, whose thickness gives synchronism its con-
sistency, and lacking which synchronism would
dissolve into a tenuous and impalpable essence, a
phantom of reality.

It would thus not be over-bold to suggest that in its
oral expression, the teaching of de Saussure must not
have been very far from these profound remarks by
Durkheim, which, published in 1900, seem to have
been written today :

> Without a doubt, the phenomena which concern
> structure are somewhat more stable than func-
> tional phenomena, but between the two orders
> of facts there is only a difference of degree.
> Structure itself occurs in the process of becom-

29

ing ... it takes shape and breaks down cease-lessly, it is life which has reached a certain degree of consolidation; and to distinguish the life whence it derives from the life which it determines would be to dissociate inseparable things.[1]

In truth, it is the nature of the facts we study which leads us to distinguish within them that which be-longs to the order of structure and that which belongs to the order of event. Important as the historical per-spective may be, we can only attain it at the end: after long researches which – as radiocarbon dating and palynology demonstrate – are not even always within our competence. By contrast, the diversity of human societies and their number – several thou-sand still at the end of the nineteenth century – make it seem to us as if they were displayed in the present. There is no cause for surprise, then, if we take a cue from our object of study and adopt a *transforma-tional* rather than a *fluxional* method.

As a matter of fact, there is a very close relation-ship between the concept of transformation and the concept of structure which is so important in our work. Radcliffe-Brown, inspired by the ideas of Mon-tesquieu and Spencer, introduced the latter into social anthropology, to designate that lasting manner in which individuals and groups are connected within the social body. For him, consequently, structure is

[1] 'La sociologie et son domaine scientifique', in *Où va la soci-ologie française?* (Paris, 1953), p. 190.

of the order of fact; it is given in the observation of each particular society. This view proceeds, no doubt, from a certain conception of the natural sciences, but one which would have already been unacceptable for a Cuvier.

No science today can consider the structures with which it has to deal as being no more than a haphazard arrangement. That arrangement alone is structured which meets two conditions: that it be a system, ruled by an internal cohesiveness; and that this cohesiveness, inaccessible to observation in an isolated system, be revealed in the study of transformations, through which the similar properties in apparently different systems are brought to light. As Goethe wrote:

All forms are similar, and none are the same,
So that their chorus points the way to a hidden law.

This convergence of scientific perspectives is very comforting for the semiological sciences in which social anthropology is included. Signs and symbols can only function in so far as they belong to systems, regulated by internal laws of implication and exclusion, and the property of a system of signs is to be transformable, in other words, *translatable*, in the language of another system with the aid of permutations. That such a conception should be born in palaeontology leads social anthropology to harbour a secret dream: it belongs to the human sciences, as its name adequately proclaims; but if it resigns itself to a period in purgatory beside the social sciences, it is because it does not despair of awakening among the natural sciences when the last trumpet sounds.

I shall attempt to show by two examples how social anthropology now endeavours to justify its programme.

We know how incest prohibitions function in primitive societies. By casting sisters and daughters out of the consanguineal group, so to speak, and by assigning them to husbands who belong to other groups, the prohibition of incest creates bonds of alliance between these biological groups, the first such bonds which one can call social. The incest prohibition is thus the basis of human society: in a sense it is the society.

We did not proceed inductively to justify this interpretation. How could we have done, with phenomena which are universally correlated, but among which different societies have posited all sorts of curious connections? Moreover, this is not a matter of facts but of meanings. The question we asked ourselves was that of the *meaning* of the incest prohibition (the eighteenth century would have said 'its spirit'), not the meaning of its *results*, real or imaginary. It was necessary, then, to establish the systematic nature of each kinship terminology and its corresponding set of marriage rules. And this was made possible only by the additional effort of elaborating the system of these systems and of putting them into transformational relationship. From then on what had been merely a huge and disordered scene became organized in grammatical terms involving a coercive charter for all conceivable ways of setting up and maintaining a reciprocity system.

This is where we are now. How then should we proceed to answer the next question: that of the universality of these rules in the totality of human societies, including contemporary ones? Even if we do not define the incest prohibition in Australian or Amerindian terms, does the form it takes among us still have the same function? It could be that we remain attached to it for very different reasons, such as the relatively recent discovery of the harmful consequences of consanguineal unions. It could also be – as Durkheim thought – that the institution no longer plays a positive role among us and that it survives only as a vestige of obsolete beliefs, anchored in popular lore. Or, is it not rather the case that our society, a particular instance in a much vaster family of societies, depends, like all others, for its coherence and its very existence on a network – grown infinitely unstable and complicated among us – of ties between consanguineal families? If so, do we have to admit that the network is homogeneous in all its parts, or must we recognize therein types of structures differing according to environment or region and variable as a function of local historical traditions?

These problems are essential for anthropology, since the response to them will determine the innermost nature of the social fact and its degree of plasticity. Now, it is impossible to settle this once and for all by using methods borrowed from the logic of John Stuart Mill. We cannot vary the complex relationships – on the technical, economic, professional, political, religious and *biological* planes – which a contemporary society presupposes. We cannot interrupt and re-establish them at will in the hope of discovering which ones are indispensable to the existence of the society as such, and which ones it could do without if it had to.

However, we could choose the most complex and least stable of those matrimonial systems whose reciprocity function is best established. We could then construct models of them in the laboratory to determine how they would function if they involved increasing numbers of individuals; we could also distort our models in the hope of obtaining others of the same type but even more complex and unstable; and we could compare the reciprocity cycles thus obtained with the simplest cycles it is possible to observe in the field among contemporary societies, e.g., in regions characterized by small isolates. Through a series of trips from laboratory to field and field to laboratory, we would try gradually to fill in the gap between two series – one known, the other unknown – by the insertion of a series of intermediary forms. In the end, we would have done nothing but elaborate a language whose only virtues, as in the case of any language, would reside in its coherence and its ability to account, in terms of a very small number of rules, for phenomena thought to be very different until that moment. In the absence of an inaccessible factual truth, we would have arrived at a truth of reason.

The second example relates to problems of the same type approached on another level: it will still be concerned with the incest prohibition, but no longer in the form of a system of rules – rather, in the form of a theme for mythical thought.

34

The Iroquois and Algonquin Indians tell the story of a young girl subjected to the amorous leanings of a nocturnal visitor whom she believes to be her brother. Everything seems to point to the guilty one : physical appearance, clothing, and the scratched cheek which bears witness to the heroine's virtue. Formally accused by her, the brother reveals that he has a counterpart or, more exactly, a double, for the tie between them is so strong that any accident befalling the one is automatically transmitted to the other. To convince his incredulous sister, the young man kills his double before her, but at the same time he condemns himself, since their destinies are linked.

Of course, the mother of the victim will want to avenge her son. As it happens she is a powerful sorceress, the mistress of the owls. There is only one way of misleading her : that the sister marry her brother, the latter passing for the double he has killed. Incest is so inconceivable that the old woman never suspects the hoax. The owls are not fooled and denounce the guilty ones, but they succeed in escaping.

The Western listener easily perceives in this myth a theme established by the Oedipus legend : the very precautions taken to avoid incest in fact make it inevitable; in both cases a sensational turn of events arises from the fact that two characters, originally introduced as distinct, are identified with each other. Is this simply a coincidence – different causes explaining the fact that the same motifs are arbitrarily found together – or does the analogy have deeper foundations? In making the comparison, have we not put our finger on a fragment of a meaningful whole?

If so, the incest between brother and sister of the Iroquois myth would constitute a permutation of the Oedipal incest between mother and son. The contingency which rendered the former inevitable – the double personality of the hero – would be a permutation of the double identity of Oedipus – supposed dead and nevertheless living, condemned child and triumphant hero. To complete the demonstration, it would be necessary to discover in the American myth a transformation of the sphinx episode, which is the only element of the Oedipus legend still lacking.

Now, in this particular case (and hence we have chosen it in preference to others), the proof would be truly decisive, since, as Boas was the first to point out, riddles or puzzles, along with proverbs, are rather rare among the North American Indians. If puzzles *were* to be found in the semantic framework of the American myth, it would not be the effect of chance, but a proof of necessity.

In the whole of North America only two puzzle situations are found whose origins are unquestionably indigenous: (1) among the Pueblo Indians of the south-western United States we have a family of ceremonial clowns who set riddles to the spectators and whom myths describe as having been born of an incestuous union; and (2) precisely among the Algonquin themselves (remember that the sorceress in the myth summarized here is a mistress of owls), there are myths in which owls, or sometimes the ancestor of owls, set riddles to the hero which he must answer under pain of death. Consequently, in America too, riddles present a double Oedipal character: by way of incest, on the one hand, and by way of the owl, in which we are led to see a transposed form of the sphinx, on the other.

The correlation between riddle and incest thus seems to obtain among peoples separated by history, geography, language and culture. In order to set up the comparison, let us construct a model of the riddle, expressing as best we can its constant properties throughout the various mythologies. Let us define it, from this point of view, as *a question to which one postulates that there is no answer*. Without considering here all the possible transformations of this statement, let us simply, by way of an experiment, invert its terms. This produces *an answer for which there is no question*.

This is, apparently, a formula completely devoid of sense. And yet, it is immediately obvious that there are myths, or fragments of myths, which derive their dramatic power from this structure – a symmetrical inversion of the other. Time is too limited for me to recount the American examples, I will therefore restrict myself to reminding you of the death of the Buddha, rendered inevitable because a disciple fails to ask the expected question. Closer to home, there are the old myths refurbished in the Holy Grail cycle, in which the action depends on the timidity of the hero. In the presence of the magic vessel he dare not ask, 'What is it good for?'

Are these myths independent, or must they be considered in turn as a species of a vaster genus, of which Oedipal myths constitute only another species? Repeating the procedure we have described, we will see if, and to what extent, the characteristic elements of one group can be reduced to permutations (which will here be inversions) of the characteristic elements of the other. And that indeed is what takes place : from a hero who misuses sexual intercourse (since he carries it as far as incest), we pass on to a chaste man who abstains from it; a shrewd person who knows all the answers gives way to an innocent who is not even aware of the need to ask questions. In the American variants of this second type, and in the Holy Grail cycle, the problem to be resolved is that of the '*gaste pays*', that is to say, the cancelled summer. Now, all the American myths of the first or 'Oedipal' type refer to an eternal winter which the hero dispels when he solves the puzzles, thereby bringing on the summer. Simplifying a great deal, Perceval thus appears as an inverted Oedipus – a hypothesis we would not have dared to consider had we been called upon to compare a Greek with a Celtic source, but which is forced upon us in a North American context, where the two types are present in the same population.

However, we have not reached the end of our demonstration. As soon as we have verified that, in a semantic system, chastity is related to 'the answer without a question' as incest is related to 'the question without an answer', we must also admit that the two socio-biological statements are themselves in a homologous relation to the two grammatical statements. Between the puzzle solution and incest there exists a relationship, not external and of fact, but internal and of reason, and that indeed is why civilizations as different as those of classical antiquity and indigenous America can independently associate the two. Like the solved puzzle, incest brings together

38

elements doomed to remain separate: the son marries the mother, the brother marries the sister, *in the same way in which the answer succeeds, against all expectations, in getting back to its question.*

In the legend of Oedipus, then, marriage with Jocasta does not arbitrarily follow hard upon victory over the sphinx. Besides the fact that myths of the Oedipal type (which this argument defines fairly precisely) always assimilate the discovery of incest to the solution of a living puzzle personified by the hero, their various episodes are repeated on different levels and in different languages and provide the same demonstration which one finds in an inverted form in the old myths of the Holy Grail. The audacious union of masked words or of consanguines unknown to themselves engenders decay and fermentation, the unchaining of natural forces – one thinks of the Theban plague – just as impotence in sexual matters (and in the ability to initiate a proposed dialogue) dries up animal and vegetable fertility.

In the face of the two possibilities which might seduce the imagination – an eternal summer or a winter just as eternal, the former licentious to the point of corruption, the latter pure to the point of sterility – man must resign himself to choosing equilibrium and the periodicity of the seasonal rhythm. In the natural order, the latter fulfils the same function which is fulfilled in society by the exchange of women in marriage and the exchange of words in conversation, when these are practised with the frank intention of communicating, that is to say, without trickery or perversity, and above all, without hidden motives.

* * *

39

I have been satisfied simply to sketch in the broad outlines of a demonstration – which will be taken up again in detail on some future occasion – to illustrate this problem of invariance which social anthropology seeks to resolve. The other sciences are concerned with this problem too, but for anthropology it seems like the modern form of a question with which it has always been concerned – that of the universality of human nature. Do we not turn our backs on this human nature when, in order to sift out our invariants, we replace the data of experience with models upon which we are free to perform abstract operations as the algebrist does with his equations? I have sometimes been reproached with this. Apart from the fact, however, that the objection carries little weight with the expert – who knows with what fastidious fidelity to concrete reality he pays for the liberty of skimming for a few brief moments – I would like to remind you that in proceeding as it does, social anthropology is only reassuming responsibility for a forgotten part of the programme which Durkheim and Mauss mapped out.

In the preface to the second edition of *The Rules of Sociological Method*, Durkheim defends himself against the charge of having unjustifiably separated the collective from the individual. This separation, he says, is necessary, but it does not preclude the possibility that in the future,

we will come to conceive of the possibility of a completely formal psychology which would be a sort of common ground of individual psychology and sociology ... what would be necessary would be to seek, by the comparison of mythic themes, legends, popular traditions, and languages, in what way social representations call for each other or are mutually exclusive, merge with one another or remain distinct ... (Durkheim, 1960: viii–xix).

This research, he noted in closing, pertains on the whole to the field of abstract logic. It is curious to note in passing how close Lévy-Bruhl could have come to this programme if he had not chosen at the outset to relegate mythic representations to the antechamber of logic, and if he had not rendered the separation irremediable when he later renounced the notion of prelogical thought. In so doing, he was simply throwing out the baby with the bathwater: he denied to 'primitive mentality' the cognitive character which he had initially conceded to it, and cast it back entirely into the realm of affectivity.

More faithful to the Durkheimian conception of an 'obscure psychology' underlying social reality, Mauss orients anthropology 'towards the study of what men have in common ... Men communicate by symbols ... but they can only have these symbols and communicate by them because they have the same instincts.'[1]

Such a conception, which is also my own, may well lend itself to another form of criticism. If your final goal is to arrive at certain universal forms of thought and morality (and the *Essay on the Gift* does end with conclusions on morals), why ascribe a privileged

[1] 'Rapports réels et pratiques de la psychologie et de la sociologie'. in *Sociologie et Anthropologie* (Paris, 1950), p. 296.

status to the societies which you call primitive? Shouldn't one in theory arrive at the same results by starting from any society? This is the final problem which I would like to consider here.

It is all the more vital to do so since some anthropologists and sociologists who study societies in rapid transformation will perhaps dispute the ideas which I seem implicitly to have about primitive societies. The distinctive characteristics which I impute to them, they may believe, verge on an illusion which is the effect of our present ignorance of what is actually going on. Objectively, they do not correspond to reality.

Without a doubt, the character of ethnographic investigation is changing as the little savage tribes we used to study disappear and are absorbed into larger entities whose problems come to resemble our own. But if it is true, as Mauss taught us, that anthropology is an original mode of knowing rather than a source of particular types of knowledge, we can only conclude that today anthropology is conducted in two ways: in the pure state and in the diluted state. To seek to develop it where its method is mixed with other methods, where its object is confused with other objects, is not the course of action resulting from a sound scientific attitude. This chair will therefore be devoted to pure anthropology. I do not mean that its teaching cannot be applied to other ends, nor that it is uninterested in contemporary societies, which, at certain levels and from certain points of view, are immediately relevant to anthropological method.

What, then, *are* the reasons for our concentration

on those societies, which, in the absence of a better term, we call primitive, although they certainly are not that?

The first reason, let us be straightforward about it, is of a philosophical order. As Merleau-Ponty has written,

> each time the sociologist (but it is the anthropologist he is *thinking of*) returns to the living sources of his knowledge, to that which operates in him as a means of understanding the cultural formations most remote from himself, he is spontaneously indulging in philosophy.[1]

And, indeed, the field research with which every anthropological career begins is the mother and wet-nurse of doubt, the philosophical attitude par excellence. This 'anthropological doubt' does not only consist of knowing that one knows nothing, but of resolutely exposing what one thought one knew, and indeed one's very own ignorance, to the buffetings and denials which are directed at one's most cherished ideas and habits by other ideas and habits which must needs contradict them to the highest degree. Contrary to appearances, I think it is by its more strictly philosophical method that anthropology is distinguished from sociology. The sociologist objectivizes for fear of being misled. The anthropologist does not experience this fear, since he is not immediately concerned in the distant society he studies and since he is not compelled in advance to leave out of consideration all its nuances, details, and even values – in a

[1] 'Le philosophe et le sociologue', in *Signes* (Paris, 1960), p. 138.

word: all that in which an observer of his own society risks being implicated.

However, in choosing a subject and an object radically distant from one another, anthropology runs a risk: that the knowledge obtained from the object does not attain its intrinsic properties but is limited to expressing the relative and always shifting position of the subject in relation to that object. It may very well be, indeed, that so-called ethnological knowledge is condemned to remain as bizarre and inadequate as that which an exotic visitor would have of our own society. The Kwakiutl Indian whom Boas sometimes invited to New York to serve him as an informant was quite indifferent to the panorama of skyscrapers and of streets ploughed and furrowed by cars. He reserved all his intellectual curiosity for the dwarfs, giants and bearded ladies who were exhibited in Times Square at the time, for automats, and for the brass balls decorating staircase banisters. For reasons which I cannot go into here, all these things challenged his own culture, and it was that culture alone which he was seeking to recognize in certain aspects of ours.

In their own way, do not anthropologists succumb to the same temptation when they permit themselves, as they so often do, to re-interpret indigenous customs and institutions with the unacknowledged aim of making them square more adequately with the latest body of theory? The problem of totemism, which some of us hold to be transparent and insubstantial, has weighed upon anthropological thinking for years, and we understand now that its importance proceeds from a certain taste for the obscene and the grotesque which is for the science of religion like a childhood disease : a negative projection of an uncontrollable fear of the sacred from which the observer has not been able to disengage himself. Thus the theory of totemism is set up 'for us', not 'in itself', and nothing guarantees that in its current form it does not still proceed from a similar illusion.

The anthropologists of my generation are disconcerted by Frazer's aversion to the research he had done all his life : 'tragic chronicles', he wrote, 'of the errors of man : foolish, vain efforts, wasted time, frustrated hopes.'[1] We are hardly less surprised to learn from the *Notebooks* how a Lévy-Bruhl considered myths, which, according to him, 'no longer have any effect on us ... strange narratives, not to say absurd and incomprehensible ... it costs us an effort to take an interest in them ... ' Of course, we have acquired direct knowledge of exotic forms of life and thought which our precursors lacked; but is it not also the case that surrealism – an internal development of our own society – has transformed our sensitivity, and that we are indebted to it for having discovered or rediscovered at the heart of our studies a certain lyricism and integrity ?

Let us then resist the appeal of a naive objectivism, but without failing to recognize that, by its very precariousness, our position as observers brings us unhoped-for guarantees of objectivity. It is to the extent that so-called primitive societies are very distant from our own, that we can discover in them those 'facts of general functioning' of which Mauss

[1] *Aftermath. A Supplement to the Golden Bough* (London, 1936), p. vi.

spoke, which stand a chance of being 'more universal' and 'more real'.[1] In these societies – I am still quoting Mauss – 'one grasps individuals, groups – and behaviour ... one sees them driven as in a piece of machinery ... one sees agglomerations and systems'.[2] This observation, privileged by distance, no doubt implies certain differences in nature between these societies and our own. Astronomy requires not only that celestial bodies be distant, but also that the passage of time there should have a different rhythm. Otherwise, the earth would have ceased to exist long before astronomy was born.

So-called primitive societies, of course, exist in history; their past is as old as ours, since it goes back to the origin of the species. Over thousands of years they have undergone all sorts of transformations; they have known wars, migrations, adventure. But they have specialized in ways different from those which we have chosen. Perhaps they have, in certain respects, remained closer to very ancient conditions of life, but this does not preclude the possibility that in other respects they are farther from those conditions than we are.

Although they exist in history, these societies seem to have elaborated or retained a particular wisdom which incites them to resist desperately any structural modification which would afford history a point of

[1] Lucien Lévy-Bruhl, *Les Carnets de Lucien Lévy-Bruhl* (Paris, 1949), p. 200.
[2] 'Essai sur le don', p. 276.

entry into their lives. Those which have best protected their distinctive character appear to be societies predominantly concerned with persevering in their existence. The way in which they exploit the environment guarantees both a modest standard of living and the conservation of natural resources. Their marriage rules, though varied, reveal to the eye of the demographer a common function, namely to set the fertility rate very low and to keep it constant. Finally, a political life based on consent, and admitting of no decisions other than those unanimously arrived at, seems conceived to preclude the possibility of calling on that driving force of collective life which takes advantage of the contrast between power and opposition, majority and minority, exploiter and exploited.

In a word, these societies, which we might define as 'cold' in that their internal environment neighbours on the zero of historical temperature, are, by their limited total manpower and their mechanical mode of functioning, distinguished from the 'hot' societies which appeared in different parts of the world following the Neolithic revolution. In these, differentiations between castes and between classes are urged unceasingly in order to extract social change and energy from them.

The value of this distinction is mainly theoretical: it is unlikely that any society can be found which would correspond exactly to one or the other type. And in another sense also the distinction remains relative, if it is true, as I believe, that social anthropology responds to a double motivation. First: retrospective, since the various types of primitive life are on the point of disappearing and we must hasten to cull our lessons from them. Second: prospective, to the extent that, being conscious of an evolution whose tempo is constantly accelerating, we experience ourselves already as the 'primitives' of our great-grandchildren, so that we seek to validate ourselves by drawing closer to those who were – and still are, for a brief moment – like a part of us which persists in its existence.

On the other hand, neither do those societies which I have called 'hot' manifest this character to an absolute degree. When, on the morrow of the Neolithic revolution, the great city-states of the Mediterranean Basin and of the Far East perpetrated slavery, they constructed a type of society in which the differential statuses of men – some dominant, others dominated – could be used to produce culture at a rate until then inconceivable and unthought of. By the same logic, the industrial revolution of the nineteenth century represents less an evolution oriented in the same direction, than a rough sketch of a different solution: though for a long time it remained based on the same abuses and injustices, yet it made possible the transfer to *culture* of that dynamic function which the protohistoric revolution had assigned to *society*.

If – Heaven forbid! – it were expected of the anthropologist that he predict the future of humanity, he would undoubtedly not conceive of it as a continuation or a projection of present types, but rather on the model of an integration, progressively unifying the appropriate characteristics of the 'cold' societies and the 'hot' ones. His thought would renew connections with the old Cartesian dream of putting machines, like automatons, at the service of man. It would follow this lead through the social philosophy of the eighteenth century and up to Saint-Simon. The latter, in announcing the passage 'from government of men to the administration of things', anticipated in the same breath the anthropological distinction between culture and society. He thus looked forward to an event of which advances in information theory and electronics give us at least a glimpse: the conversion of a type of civilization which inaugurated historical development at the price of the transformation of men into machines into an ideal civilization which would succeed in turning machines into men. Then, culture having entirely taken over the burden of manufacturing progress, society would be freed from the millennial curse which has compelled it to enslave men in order that there be progress. Henceforth, history would make itself by itself. Society, placed outside and above history, would be able to exhibit once again that regular and, as it were, crystalline structure which the best-preserved of primitive societies teach us is not antagonistic to the human condition. In this perspective, utopian as it might seem, social anthropology would find its highest justification, since the forms of life and thought which it studies would no longer have a purely historical or comparative interest. They would correspond to a permanent hope for mankind over which social anthropology, particularly in the most troubled times, would have a mission to keep watch.

Our science would not have been able to stand as a sentinel in this way – and would not even have conceived of the importance and the necessity of it –

if, on the remote borders of the earth, men had not obstinately resisted history, and if they had not remained as living testimonials of that which we want to preserve.

In conclusion, I should very much like to describe in a few words the very exceptional emotion which the anthropologist experiences when he enters a house in which tradition, uninterrupted for four centuries, goes back to the reign of Francis I. For an Americanist, especially, how many ties link him with that age in which the New World was revealed to Europe by being laid open to ethnographical inquiry! He would have wanted to live then – indeed, he does so every day in his thoughts. And because, very remarkably, the Indians of Brazil (among whom I took my first steps in our discipline) could have adopted as a motto 'I will maintain', it happens that their study takes on a double quality: that of a journey to a distant land, and – even more mysterious – that of an exploration of the past.

But for this reason also – and bearing in mind the fact that the mission of the Collège de France has always been to teach science in the making – I can hardly repress a pang of regret. Why was this chair created so late? How does it happen that anthropology did not receive its due when it was still young, and when the facts still retained their richness and freshness? For it is in 1558 that one likes to imagine this chair being established, when Jean de Léry, returning from Brazil, drafted his first work, and when

André Thevet's *The Singularities of French Antarctica* appeared.

Social anthropology would certainly be more respectable and self-assured today if official recognition had been granted at the moment when it was beginning to formulate its intentions. Supposing, however, that all had come to pass in this way, anthropology would not be what it is today : a restless and fervent study which plagues the investigator with moral as well as scientific questions. It was perhaps in the nature of our science that it should appear at one and the same moment as an effort to make up for lost time and as a reflection on a discrepancy to which certain of its fundamental characteristics should be attributed.

If society is in anthropology, anthropology is itself in society : it has been able to enlarge progressively the object of its study to the point of including therein the totality of human societies : although it has appeared at a late period in their history and in a small sector of the inhabited world. More than that, the circumstances of its appearance are comprehensible only in the context of a particular social and economic development : one suspects, then, that they go together with a dawning awareness – almost remorseful – that humanity could have remained alienated from itself for such a long time, and above all, that that fraction of humanity which produced anthropology should be the same fraction of humanity to have made so many other men the objects of execration and contempt. 'Sequels to colonialism', it is sometimes said of our investigations. The two are certainly linked, but nothing would be more misleading than to see anthropology as a throwback to the colonial frame of mind, a shameful ideology which would offer colonialism a chance of survival.

What we call the Renaissance was a veritable birth for colonialism and for anthropology. Between the two, confronting each other from the time of their common origin, an equivocal dialogue has been pursued for four centuries. If colonialism had not existed, the elaboration of anthropology would have been less belated; but perhaps also anthropology would not have been led to implicate all mankind in each of its particular case-studies. Our science arrived at maturity the day that Western man began to see that he would never understand himself as long as there was a single race or people on the surface of the earth that he treated as an object. Only then could anthropology declare itself in its true colours: as an enterprise reviewing and atoning for the Renaissance, in order to spread humanism to all humanity.

After rendering homage to the masters of social anthropology at the beginning of this lecture, let me devote my last words to those 'primitives' whose modest tenacity still offers us a means of assigning to human facts their true dimensions. Men and women who, as I speak, thousands of miles from here on some savannah ravaged by brush fire, or in some forest under torrential rain, are returning to camp to share a meagre pittance and to invoke their gods together; those Indians of the tropics and their counterparts throughout the world who have taught me their humble knowledge (in which is contained, neverthless, the essence of the knowledge which my colleagues have charged me to transmit to others): soon, alas, they are all destined for extinction under the impact of illnesses and – for them even more horrible – modes of life with which we have plagued them. To them I have incurred a debt which I can never repay, even if, in the place in which you have put me, I were able to give some proof of the tenderness which they inspire in me and of the gratitude which I feel towards them by continuing to be as I was among them, and as, among you, I would hope never to cease from being : their pupil, their witness.

SELECTED BIBLIOGRAPHY

A list of the principal works of Claude Lévi-Strauss,
with the dates of their first appearance

LA VIE FAMILIALE ET SOCIALE DES INDIENS
NAMBIKWARA
(Société des Américanistes, Paris, 1948)

LES STRUCTURES ÉLÉMENTAIRES DE LA
PARENTÉ
(Presses Universitaires de France, 1949)

'INTRODUCTION À L'ŒUVRE DE MARCEL MAUSS',
in M. Mauss, SOCIOLOGIE ET ANTHROPOLOGIE
(P.U.F., 1950)

RACE ET HISTOIRE
(UNESCO, 1952), translated as RACE AND
HISTORY (UNESCO, 1952)

TRISTES TROPIQUES
(Plon, 1958), translated as WORLD ON THE WANE
(Hutchinson, 1961)

ANTHROPOLOGIE STRUCTURALE
(Plon, 1958), translated as STRUCTURAL
ANTHROPOLOGY (Basic Books, New York, 1963)

'LA GESTE D'ASDIWAL'
(ANNUAIRE DE L'ÉCOLE PRATIQUE DES
HAUTES ÉTUDES, 5ième Section, 1958–9, 1960),
translated as 'THE STORY OF ASDIWAL', in E.
Leach (editor), THE STRUCTURAL STUDY OF
MYTH AND TOTEMISM (Tavistock Publications,
1967)

ENTRETIENS AVEC CLAUDE LÉVI-STRAUSS (with
Georges Charbonnier), (Plon-Julliard, 1961)

LE TOTÉMISME AUJOURD'HUI
(P.U.F., 1962), translated as TOTEMISM (Merlin
Press, 1964)

LA PENSÉE SAUVAGE
(Plon, 1962), translated as THE SAVAGE MIND
(Weidenfeld & Nicolson, 1966)

MYTHOLOGIQUES : LE CRU ET LE CUIT (Plon, 1964),
translated as THE RAW AND THE COOKED (Cape,
1971); DU MIEL AUX CENDRES (Plon, 1966), translated as FROM HONEY TO ASHES (Cape, 1972)

THE AUTHOR

Claude Lévi-Strauss was born in 1908 in Belgium and educated at the University of Paris in Philosophy and Law. From 1935 to 1939 he taught at the University of São Paulo, Brazil, and first came into contact with Amazon Indians. He served in the army in 1939. From 1942 to 1945 he worked at the New School for Social Research and the École Libre des Hautes Études in New York, subsequently becoming Cultural Attaché at the French Embassy from 1946–7. On his return to France in 1947 he became, successively, Associate Director of the Musée de l'Homme, Directeur d'Études at the École Pratique des Hautes Études and the Editor of *L'Homme, revue française d'anthropologie.* He is an Honorary Fellow : Royal Anthropological Institute of Great Britain and Ireland; Foreign Fellow : American Philosophical Society; American Academy of Arts and Sciences; Royal Academy of the Netherlands; Norwegian Academy of Science and Letters; Doctor *honoris causa* : Université Libre de Bruxelles; Yale University; Oxford University; *Officier de la Légion d'Honneur.* Since 1960, Claude Lévi-Strauss has been Professor of Social Anthropology at the Collège de France.